BIOGRA[illegible]

MICHAEL PARKINSON

BOOK

"Michael Parkinson: A Legacy Etched in Time (1935-2023)"

Nora Ivey Press

Table Of Content

Introduction

Chapter One: Early Beginnings

Chapter Two:Venturing Forth

Chapter Three: The Birth of an Icon

Chapter Four: Crafting the Format

Chapter Five: Beyond the Spotlight

Chapter Six: Unveiling the Man

Chapter Seven: Navigating Challenges, Embracing Triumphs

Chapter Eight: Net Worth and Legacy

Chapter Nine: The Final Curtain

Chapter Ten: Reflecting on a Life

Conclusion: A Lasting Impact

Introduction

The Life of a Great Journalist

Born on March 28, 1935, in Cudworth, England, Michael Parkinson's beginnings were humble. Growing up in a working-class family with a father who was a miner and a mother who was a housewife, he displayed an early fascination with journalism. His insatiable curiosity, love for reading, and knack for writing led him to embark on a remarkable journey.

Embracing the World of Journalism

At just 16 years old, Parkinson's journey into journalism commenced when he secured a role as a cub reporter for the Barnsley Chronicle. Eager to learn, he swiftly honed his skills, evolving into a proficient journalist with an innate ability to capture stories.

Setting Foot in London

In 1961, Parkinson's path led him to London, where he joined the ranks of the Sunday Times. Here, he navigated diverse subjects ranging from politics to sports and entertainment. His inquisitiveness extended to interviewing celebrities, cultivating a reputation for his adeptness as an interviewer.

The Rise of a Skilled Interviewer

1971 marked a pivotal moment when Parkinson found himself at the helm of his talk show on the BBC, aptly named "Parkinson." It swiftly soared to become a television sensation, a platform where luminaries like Muhammad Ali, Frank Sinatra, and Margaret Thatcher shared their stories. Renowned for his warm and engaging interview style, Parkinson had a remarkable knack for eliciting personal narratives from his guests.

A Household Name

Running for 11 years, "Parkinson" etched his name in households worldwide. His contributions to broadcasting were lauded with a knighthood in 1998. Although he bid farewell to his talk show in 1998, he continued his broadcast career, hosting shows such as "Parkinson on Sunday" and "Parkinson's Sunday Supplement." His literary endeavors also flourished, including the publication of his autobiography, "Parky: My Life."

Diverse Horizons

Parkinson's influence extended beyond talk shows. He ventured into radio presenting and even dabbled in acting, making appearances in films like "The Full Monty" and TV shows like "Gavin & Stacey." His philanthropic spirit shone through his role as a patron of the Parkinson's Disease Society.

Personal Bonds

In the realm of personal life, Parkinson experienced marriage twice. His union with Mary Parkinson bore three children, while his second marriage to Mary Yates brought one child into the world.

Navigating Challenges

Throughout his journey, Parkinson faced trials, including the loss of his first wife and his diagnosis of Parkinson's disease. Yet, he displayed unwavering resilience, persisting in his work and inspiring countless individuals.

A Legacy Defined

With an estimated net worth of £10 million, Parkinson left behind a profound legacy. A trailblazer in the talk show landscape, he played an instrumental role in popularizing the genre. His gift as an interviewer, capable of drawing out personal tales from guests, remains unrivaled. His enduring legacy ensures his influence resonates for generations to come.

A Farewell at 88

Tragically, on August 16, 2023, Parkinson's journey came to an end at the age of 88. Complications stemming from Parkinson's disease led to his passing.

An Everlasting Impact

Reflecting on his life, Michael Parkinson emerges as an extraordinary figure. Rising from modest beginnings, he transcended to become one of broadcasting's towering achievers. As a talk show pioneer and a masterful interviewer, he indelibly marked television history. His legacy, founded on sharing personal narratives, will echo through the ages, leaving an indelible imprint on the world of media and storytelling.

Chapter One: Early Beginnings

In the quiet town of Cudworth, England, a future icon was born on March 28, 1935. Michael Parkinson`s story began amidst modest circumstances, but the trajectory of his life was destined for greatness. The backdrop of his formative years played an integral role in shaping the man he would become.

Birth and Upbringing: A Simple Start

From the very start, Michael's life was a testament to the value of hard work and perseverance. Born into a working-class family, his father toiled as a miner while his mother dutifully cared for their home. Theirs was a life defined by humility, where each day was a testament to resilience and determination.

Exploring Family Roots: The Heart of Michael's Tale

A glimpse into Michael Parkinson's family background reveals the roots that anchored his character. The challenges his parents faced, the values they instilled, and the stories they shared all wove together to create the fabric of his identity. Their influence was the cornerstone upon which he built his dreams.

Shaping Influences: Nurturing Curiosity and Ambition

In his early years, Michael's curiosity burned bright. He was drawn to the world beyond his doorstep, eager to unravel its mysteries. His insatiable appetite for knowledge drove him to explore books and ideas beyond his years. This intellectual hunger, coupled with the guidance of mentors and teachers, paved the way for his future pursuits.

As a teenager, Michael embarked on a remarkable journey when he landed a position as a cub reporter for the Barnsley Chronicle. This entry into the world of journalism marked a pivotal moment, one that would set the course for his illustrious career. Through keen observation and an eagerness to learn, he quickly grasped the intricacies of the trade, proving his mettle as a gifted storyteller.

Michael Parkinson's early beginnings were a blend of simplicity, hard work, and an unquenchable thirst for knowledge. His family's influence, coupled with his innate curiosity, formed the foundation upon which he would build a life that resonated with people around the world. Little did he know that these early chapters would lay the groundwork for a journey marked by success, resilience, and the power of storytelling.

Chapter Two: Venturing Forth

As the winds of destiny continued to blow, young Michael Parkinson found himself standing at a crossroads. Armed with ambition and an insatiable curiosity, he set forth on a path that would lead him into the captivating world of journalism. This chapter unfolds the remarkable journey of his transition from humble origins to a trailblazing journalist, driven by a fervent passion for storytelling.

Embarking on His Path to Journalism: A Journey Unfolds

With each step he took, Michael's journey into the realm of journalism gained momentum. Inspired by the world around him and guided by an innate gift for observation, he recognized the power of words to capture life's intricacies. His desire to share these stories with the world marked the genesis of his career.

Transitioning to Professional Growth: Navigating New Horizons

From a cub reporter at the Barnsley Chronicle to the bustling streets of London, Michael's transition to professional growth was marked by determination and adaptability. His relocation to the bustling city in 1961 to join the Sunday Times marked a significant chapter in his life. The world of reporting unfolded before him, beckoning with diverse subjects ranging from politics to sports and the glitz of entertainment.

Discovering a Passion for Writing and Reporting: A Lifelong Love Affair

Amidst the tapestry of London's bustling journalism scene, Michael found his true calling: writing and reporting. His flair for weaving narratives, combined with an insatiable curiosity, set him apart as a journalist of distinction. The stories he uncovered weren't just pieces of news; they were windows into the human experience.

The interview arena became his stage, where he transformed into a masterful conductor of conversations. His encounters with celebrities and luminaries unveiled a unique skill—the ability to engage, empathize, and connect on a profound level. These interactions would become his hallmark, captivating audiences and subjects alike.

Chapter 2 paints a vivid picture of Michael Parkinson's foray into the world of journalism. It was a journey marked by transition—transcending from a young, curious mind to a professional captivated by the stories of the world. The passion for storytelling that ignited within him set the stage for his future, laying the foundation for the indelible mark he would make in the realm of media and broadcasting.

Chapter Three: The Birth of an Icon

In the annals of broadcasting history, a defining moment awaited Michael Parkinson—a moment that would see the birth of an iconic talk show that would etch his name in the cultural tapestry. Chapter three unveils the inception and evolution of the "Parkinson" talk show, delves into the distinctive conversational style that became his signature, and uncovers the initial challenges and triumphant breakthroughs that marked his journey into the realm of talk show stardom.

The Inception and Evolution of the "Parkinson" Talk Show: A Phenomenon Unfolds

The canvas of British television was forever altered when "Parkinson" premiered. The seeds of this groundbreaking show were sown in 1971 when Michael's vision for an engaging and insightful platform bore fruit. Each episode showcased riveting conversations with some of the world's most illustrious figures, be they celebrities, political luminaries, or cultural icons.

As the show evolved, it became a melting pot of candid exchanges and heartfelt revelations. It wasn't just another talk show—it was a portal into the lives, thoughts, and experiences of those who graced its stage. The "Parkinson" talk show set the standard for compelling, unfiltered interviews that would stand the test of time.

Examining the Impact of His Conversational Style: A Masterclass in Dialogue

Central to the show's success was Michael's unique conversational style. His warmth, wit, and ability to put guests at ease fostered an environment where they could open up in ways rarely seen on television. The art of conversation became a dance, guided by his adeptness in eliciting candid insights from even the most reticent guests.

The show wasn't a mere Q&A session—it was a platform for genuine connection. Michael's genuine curiosity, empathy, and knack for reading between the lines turned interviews into captivating dialogues that resonated with audiences worldwide.

Initial Challenges and Triumphs in the Talk Show Arena: Forging Ahead

Yet, the journey to becoming a talk show icon wasn't without its trials. Initial challenges ranged from securing notable guests to navigating the logistics of production. Michael's resilience and determination, however, proved insurmountable. As each episode aired, the show's impact grew, validating his approach and fortitude.

Triumphs began to accumulate as episodes unfolded. The show garnered critical acclaim and dedicated viewership. It became a platform where legends like Muhammad Ali, Frank Sinatra, and Margaret Thatcher shared their stories—a testament to Michael's ability to breach barriers and connect with individuals from all walks of life.

paints a vivid portrait of the "Parkinson" talk show's emergence from its nascent stages into a cultural phenomenon. Michael's distinct conversational style proved to be a game-changer, revolutionizing the art of interviewing. Through initial obstacles and eventual triumphs, the "Parkinson" show became a window into the souls of those who graced its stage, a testament to Michael's prowess in the realm of broadcast conversation.

Chapter Four: Crafting the Format

Within the framework of the "Parkinson" talk show's success lies an intricate tapestry of planning, preparation, and innovation. This chapter delves into the anatomy of the show's structure and format, offering a glimpse into the meticulous art of preparing for interviews and fostering engaging conversations. Moreover, it lifts the curtain to reveal the often-unseen realm of production and direction that shaped the show's captivating aura.

Delving into the Structure and Format of the "Parkinson" Show: Designing an Experience

The "Parkinson" show was more than a mere platform; it was a meticulously designed experience. The structure itself was a delicate balance of engaging anecdotes, candid revelations, and thought-provoking insights. Each segment was thoughtfully crafted to maximize the impact of the guest's presence, ensuring that the audience would be both entertained and enlightened.

From the opening moments to the grand finale, every element was strategically positioned to create a seamless flow, inviting viewers on an immersive journey through the guest's life and thoughts.

The Art of Preparing for Interviews and Engaging Guests: A Collaborative Effort

Behind the charisma and rapport lay the result of extensive preparation. Michael's approach was anchored in thorough research, as he delved deep into each guest's background, achievements, and aspirations. Armed with a wealth of information, he embarked on a quest to elicit candid anecdotes and reveal the layers beneath the public persona.

The artistry of the interviews extended beyond Michael alone; it was a collaborative effort that involved producers, researchers, and the show's crew. The collective goal was to curate a platform that honored the guest's narrative while fostering an atmosphere of trust and comfort—a hallmark that differentiated the "Parkinson" show.

Behind-the-Scenes Insights into Production and Direction: Nurturing the Show's Essence

While the magic unfolded on screen, the orchestration backstage was a symphony of collaboration. Producers meticulously orchestrated each episode, ensuring that lighting, staging, and pacing harmonized to create an immersive experience. The director's keen eye navigated the ebb and flow of emotions, capturing the heart of each conversation.

The show's direction was a dance of intuition and precision, enhancing the guest's narrative while maintaining the authenticity that defined the "Parkinson" brand.

Chapter Four unravels the intricate threads that wove the "Parkinson" talk show's format and structure. It was a delicate fusion of planning, research, and artistic finesse. The result was an immersive journey for both guests and viewers, where storytelling flourished and human connections were forged. From concept to execution, the crafting of each episode showcased the dedication and collaborative spirit that underpinned the show's enduring impact.

Chapter Five: Beyond the Spotlight

While the "Parkinson" talk show solidified Michael's status as an icon, his influence extended far beyond the spotlight's glare. This chapter delves into his ventures that reached beyond the talk show realm, exploring his diverse forays into television projects, his immersion in the world of writing and journalism, and the multifaceted endeavors that showcased his creative prowess.

Expanding His Reach Beyond the Talk Show: A Multifaceted Journey

Michael's presence wasn't confined to the talk show stage; it resonated through a spectrum of television projects. His engaging persona and ability to connect with audiences made him a natural choice for hosting endeavors that ranged from entertainment specials to insightful documentaries. Each venture was a brushstroke that colored his canvas of influence in the world of television.

Diving into Other Television Projects and Endeavors: A Creative Odyssey

As a testament to his versatility, Michael dived into a myriad of television projects that spanned genres and themes. From captivating travel documentaries that unveiled hidden corners of the world to hosting quiz shows that blended knowledge with entertainment, he showcased a dynamic range that captivated audiences and demonstrated his adaptability as a broadcaster.

Venturing into the World of Writing and Journalism: Penning His Legacy

Michael's mastery of communication wasn't confined to spoken words alone. His literary journey paved the way for impactful contributions to the world of writing and journalism. Whether sharing personal insights in his autobiography or penning thought-provoking articles, he demonstrated artistry with the written word that mirrored his prowess in conversation.

His journey as a writer wasn't just an extension of his broadcasting persona—it was an opportunity to explore narratives, ideas, and themes in a different dimension, amplifying the resonance of his voice.

Chapter Six: Unveiling the Man

Amidst the spotlight of his illustrious career, Michael Parkinson's personal life was a tapestry woven with love, family, and the intricate threads of human relationships. Chapter Six delves into the private sphere of this broadcasting legend, shedding light on his marriages, children, and the familial bonds that defined his journey beyond the television screen.

Marriage and Partnerships: The Ties That Bind

Michael's personal life saw him embark on two significant chapters of marriage. His first union was with Mary Parkinson, a relationship that bore witness to the joys and challenges that life often presents. Together, they navigated the complexities of partnership, contributing to Michael's growth as a husband, father, and individual.

The next chapter of Michael's narrative led him to Mary Yates. Their partnership became an embodiment of shared experiences, love, and the establishment of a new family unit. The dynamics of these relationships wove a rich tapestry of companionship and shared dreams.

Fatherhood and Family: Nurturing Connections

Within the embrace of these partnerships blossomed the essence of family life. Michael's journey as a father was marked by the joys of parenting, as well as the responsibilities and joys it entails. Through the lens of fatherhood, he navigated the delicate balance between his demanding career and the nurturing of meaningful family connections.

With his first wife, Mary Parkinson, Michael welcomed three children into the world. This constellation of relationships—father to children—formed the foundation for his understanding of love, sacrifice, and the boundless support that family offers. Later, with his second wife, Mary Yates, the family unit expanded to include another child, adding another layer of love and connection.

The Heart of His Story: Love, Challenges, and Growth

Beyond the public eye, Michael's personal life was a canvas painted with hues of love, unity, and the human experiences that shape us all. His journey as a partner and father was not without its challenges, but it was through these tests that the depth of his character shone. The tapestry of his personal life was woven with threads of resilience, empathy, and an unwavering commitment to those he loved.

Chapter Six offers a glimpse into the intimate world of Michael Parkinson—the man behind the talk show host. His marriages, children, and family relationships were the pillars of support that anchored him amidst the whirlwind of his career. Through love, challenges, and growth, Michael's personal life mirrored the complexities of the human experience, revealing a multi-dimensional figure whose legacy extended beyond the realm of broadcasting.

Chapter Seven: Navigating Challenges, Embracing Triumphs

Life's journey is a tapestry woven with both challenges and triumphs. In this chapter, we delve into the trials and victories that shaped Michael Parkinson's path. From career hurdles that tested his mettle to professional achievements that illuminated his brilliance, we trace the arc of his impact on the broadcasting landscape.

Detailing Career Challenges and How He Overcame Them: Forging Ahead

Behind the glitz and glamor lay a series of challenges that tested Michael's resilience. The chapter peels back the curtain on instances where setbacks cast shadows on his journey. These challenges weren't roadblocks; they were growth opportunities. Michael's determination and unwavering spirit allowed him to navigate the treacherous terrains and emerge stronger than before.

Highlighting Professional Achievements and Milestones: Stars in His Crown

Triumphs illuminated Michael's journey, shaping a constellation of professional achievements that left an indelible mark on the world of broadcasting. The chapter highlights the moments that adorned his career with distinction—from critical acclaim to awards that testified to his excellence. His accomplishments weren't just personal; they marked milestones that redefined the standards of his craft.

Examining His Impact on the Broadcasting Landscape: A Legacy Carved in Stone

Beyond personal accomplishments, Michael's influence resonated across the broadcasting landscape. His skill as an interviewer, his ability to transcend genres, and his innate knack for fostering genuine connections defined a legacy that would be felt for generations. This chapter examines the ripple effect of his contributions, showcasing how he set the stage for future broadcasters and elevated the art of conversation.

Chapter Eight: Net Worth and Legacy

In the annals of broadcasting history, few have left an indelible mark quite like Michael Parkinson. Beyond the microphone and cameras, his legacy extended beyond the realm of storytelling—it was also reflected in his financial success. Chapter 8 sheds light on Michael's net worth, offering a glimpse into the financial landscape that mirrored his towering achievements in the world of media and entertainment.

A Wealth of Accomplishments: Financial Triumphs

As the curtains of Michael's life drew to a close, the ledger of his financial success told a tale of its own. With years of dedication and an unmatched ability to connect with audiences, he amassed a net worth that mirrored his stature as a broadcasting luminary. It was estimated that his financial worth stood at approximately £10 million—a testament to the far-reaching impact he had on the industry.

From Talk Show to Prosperity: The Business of Broadcasting

Michael's journey was a testament to the profound synergy between talent and financial recognition. The "Parkinson" show, a beacon of his prowess, was not only a platform for candid conversations—it was also a financial triumph. Its popularity resonated with viewers worldwide, paving the way for lucrative endorsements, sponsorships, and partnerships that contributed to his wealth accumulation.

Legacy Beyond Numbers: The Power of Influence

While his net worth underscored his financial accomplishments, Michael's legacy transcended mere numbers. He was a pioneer, an innovator, and a master of conversation who redefined the art of interviewing. His impact on the entertainment landscape was immeasurable, and his influence radiated far beyond monetary success.

The legacy he left behind was a testament to the culmination of dedication, passion, and unwavering commitment to his craft. His net worth, while impressive, was merely a reflection of the profound influence he wielded, one that would echo through the corridors of broadcasting history.

Chapter Eight weaves together the financial tapestry of Michael Parkinson's life, offering insight into his net worth at the time of his passing. His journey from modest beginnings to financial success mirrored his trajectory from humble reporter to celebrated talk show host. Yet, beyond the numbers, his legacy remains an inspiration—a testament to the potent fusion of talent, determination, and the enduring impact of a life well lived.

Chapter Nine: The Final Curtain

Every narrative, no matter how grand, eventually reaches its conclusion. Chapter Nine marks a somber yet essential moment as it reports the news of Michael Parkinson's passing. This chapter takes a compassionate approach, delving into the health challenges he faced in his later years, investigating the cause of his death, and reflecting on the impact of his departure.

Reporting the News of His Passing: A Solemn Farewell

Tragically, on August 16, 2023, Parkinson's journey came to an end at the age of 88. Complications stemming from Parkinson's disease led to his passing.

With heavy hearts, the world bid farewell to a broadcasting luminary. This chapter opens with the poignant news of Michael Parkinson's passing, paying tribute to a life that touched countless souls. It's an acknowledgment of the end of an era, a moment to reflect on the legacy he left behind.

Exploring the Health Challenges He Faced: A Journey of Resilience

In the twilight of his life, Michael confronted health challenges that tested his resilience. This chapter delves into these moments with empathy, exploring how he navigated the complexities of health while maintaining his characteristic spirit. It's a testament to his strength and an acknowledgment of the battles he fought with grace.

Investigating the Cause of Death and Its Impact: Seeking Understanding

The cause of Michael's passing was a complex interplay of health factors. This chapter seeks to provide insight, without sensationalism, into the medical circumstances that led to his departure. It also reflects on the impact of his passing on fans, colleagues, and the broader broadcasting community—a loss that reverberated far and wide.

Chapter Ten: Reflecting on a Life

In the tapestry of a remarkable life, Chapter Ten takes a step back to capture Michael Parkinson's insights and reflections. This chapter offers a unique glimpse into his perspective on his journey, his thoughts on his achievements, and the wisdom he gleaned from a life richly lived. It's a culmination that reverberates with his voice, sharing valuable life lessons and advice that transcend time.

Capturing Michael Parkinson's Insights and Reflections: An Intimate Dialogue

In this chapter, Michael's voice resonates as he shares intimate insights into his journey. It's a conversation that spans the highs and lows, the triumphs and tribulations, encapsulating the essence of a life well-lived. His reflections offer a personal dimension to his legacy, allowing readers to walk alongside him as he looks back on the chapters that shaped him.

His Perspective on His Journey and Achievements: A Journey Rewritten

Michael's narrative, told through his own eyes, unveils the chapters that he held closest to his heart. This chapter allows readers to witness his perspective on his professional achievements, his relationships, and the moments of growth that defined him. It's a reimagining of his journey as he revisits the pivotal junctures that led him to where he stood.

Sharing Valuable Life Lessons and Advice: Wisdom For Generations

Beyond the personal narratives, Michael's reflections are a repository of wisdom—a legacy that extends beyond his time. In this chapter, he imparts valuable life lessons, and advice garnered from the tapestry of his experiences. It's an offering to future generations, a way to continue the impact of his legacy through words of guidance, inspiration, and perspective.

Conclusion: A Lasting Impact

The final chapter draws the curtains on a narrative that traversed the life, achievements, and reflections of Michael Parkinson. This conclusion encapsulates the essence of his legacy in broadcasting and journalism, offering a panoramic view of the lasting impact he carved. It's an exploration of how his work reverberates through time, inspiring generations, and a reflection on the enduring contributions that define his name. Summarizing His Legacy in Broadcasting and Journalism: A Narrative Woven in Excellence

As the journey ends, the narrative finds its culmination in the impact Michael Parkinson made on the world of broadcasting and journalism. This chapter serves as a tapestry that weaves together the threads of his achievements, the depth of his conversations, and the innovation he brought to the craft. It's a concise encapsulation of a life lived in excellence, broadcasting history forever changed by his indelible mark.

Echoes of Influence: How His Work Continues to Inspire

The chapter isn't just a reflection; it's an acknowledgment that the story doesn't conclude with the last page. The echoes of Michael's influence continue to reverberate through generations. His innovative approach to interviews, his artistry in conversation, and his relentless pursuit of authenticity continue to inspire broadcasters, storytellers, and those who seek to make a genuine impact.

Reflections on the Enduring Contributions of Michael Parkinson: A Legacy in Motion

In the closing moments of this narrative, the chapter reflects on the enduring contributions that Michael bestowed upon the world. It contemplates how his legacy extends beyond the bounds of time, how his conversations become timeless, and his influence ripples across platforms. It's a reflection that transcends eulogy, reminding us that his legacy isn't just a memory—it's legacy in motion.

The conclusion of this journey serves as a poignant reminder that even as the narrative comes to an end, Michael Parkinson's legacy continues to unfold. It's a celebration of a life dedicated to the craft of conversation, a reflection on his impact, and an acknowledgment that his influence will forever be woven into the fabric of broadcasting and journalism. The final chapter is a bridge that connects the past, present, and future, ensuring that the story he started remains an enduring narrative of inspiration.

Printed in Great Britain
by Amazon

34039955R00036